The Library of the Five Senses & the Sixth Sense™

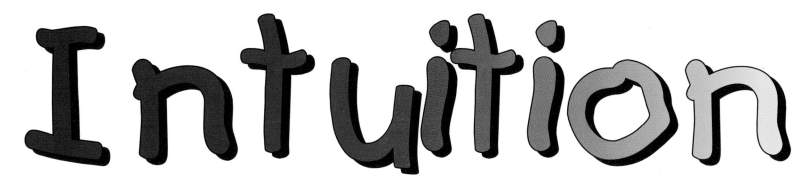

Intuition

Sue Hurwitz

The Rosen Publishing Group's
PowerKids Press™
New York

Published in 1997 by The Rosen Publishing Group, Inc.
29 East 21st Street, New York, NY 10010

First Edition

Book Design: Kim Sonsky

Photo Credits: Cover and all photo illustrations by Seth Dinnerman.

Hurwitz, Sue, 1934–
    The sixth sense: intuition / by Sue Hurwitz.
       p.   cm. — (Library of the five senses & the sixth sense)
    Includes index.
    Summary: Defines what the sixth sense, intuition, is and how it works.
    ISBN 0-8239-5057-3
    1. Intuition (Psychology)—Juvenile literature. [1. Intuition (Psychology)]
    I. Title. II. Series: Hurwitz, Sue, 1934– Library of the five senses & the sixth sense
BF315.5.H87 1997
153.4'4—dc21
                                          96–29963
                                            CIP
                                            AC

Manufactured in the United States of America

CONTENTS

What Is Intuition?

Intuition (in-too-ISH-un) is one of your **senses** (SEN-sez). Your senses tell you what is happening to you. Your senses also tell you what is happening in the world around you.

Intuition is often called your sixth sense. Sometimes it is called **instinct** (IN-stinkt) or common sense. Intuition is how your **brain** (BRAYN) uses your other five senses—taste, touch, smell, hearing, and sight—to help you know or figure out things.

4

Your intuition can help you know when to stay away from dangerous things. ▶

Nancy

Nancy used to visit her Aunt Peggy every day after school. Aunt Peggy would have milk and cookies with her while Nancy talked about her day. She loved visiting with her aunt.

Last month Aunt Peggy moved to another town. Instead of going to her aunt's house after school, Nancy went home every day. Nancy missed visiting with her aunt.

One afternoon Nancy was walking home from school. She was thinking about Aunt Peggy and how much she missed her. But she also had a feeling that she would see her aunt soon. When Nancy got to her house, she heard a familiar voice. It was Aunt Peggy! She had come for a surprise visit. Nancy's intuition about her aunt had been right.

How Does Intuition Work?

Intuition takes what you know and uses those ideas in a new way. Some people call this **insight** (IN-syt). Other people call it luck. Many people think intuition is just about being at the right place at the right time. What do you think?

You may know some things but do not know how you know them. An idea might pop into your head all of a sudden. Or you may get a feeling about something but you don't know why. For example, you may know it's not safe to walk down an empty street at night by yourself. You may not see anything dangerous, but you

just have a feeling that you should avoid that street. That's your intuition working for you.

9

How Do You Use Intuition?

Intuition can help you make good decisions and avoid bad choices. Intuition can help you stay safe.

You may have heard someone talk about "gut feelings." When you follow your gut feelings, you are finding a way to solve a problem based on what your feelings are telling you.

Decide on a problem that you want to solve. Maybe you want to do something better, such as learning how to share. Or maybe you want to get along better with a friend. Then write down your problem. Think about what you could do to solve the problem.

Following your intuition can help you think of a good way to solve the problem.

Intuition and Your Brain

Your brain makes sense out of messages that your other five senses send to it. Intuition uses these messages to make new ideas. If you're playing outside and your sense of sight tells you that it's getting dark, your intuition will tell you it's time to go home.

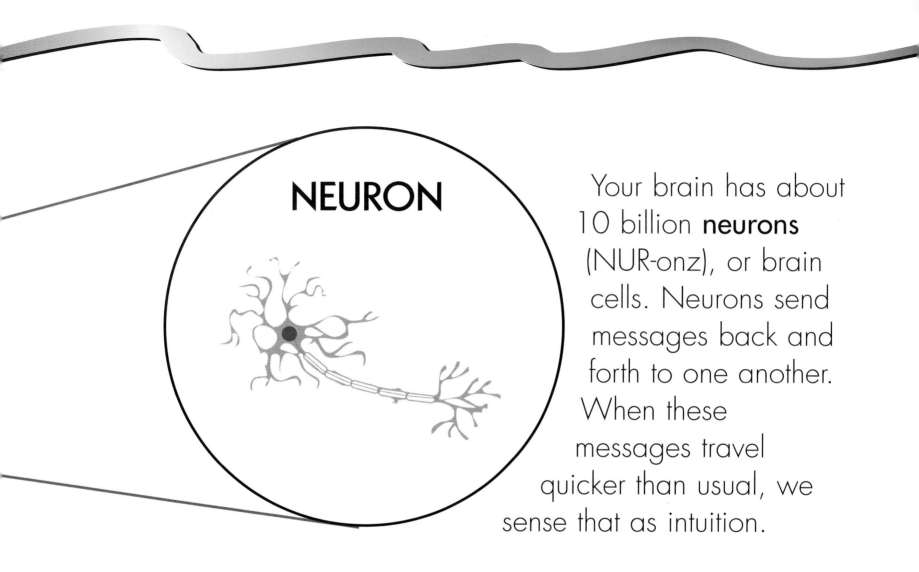

NEURON

Your brain has about 10 billion **neurons** (NUR-onz), or brain cells. Neurons send messages back and forth to one another. When these messages travel quicker than usual, we sense that as intuition.

Your Brain and Your Nervous System

Your brain is like a giant computer. It controls everything your body does. Your brain gets messages about your body from your **nerves** (NERVZ). Nerves also carry messages from your brain to other parts of your body.

Your brain is the most important part of your nervous system, which has billions of nerve cells. But each nerve cell does not work alone. Hundreds of nerve cells work together to perform a certain job in your body, such as walking up stairs, doing homework, or eating an ice cream cone.

NERVOUS SYSTEM

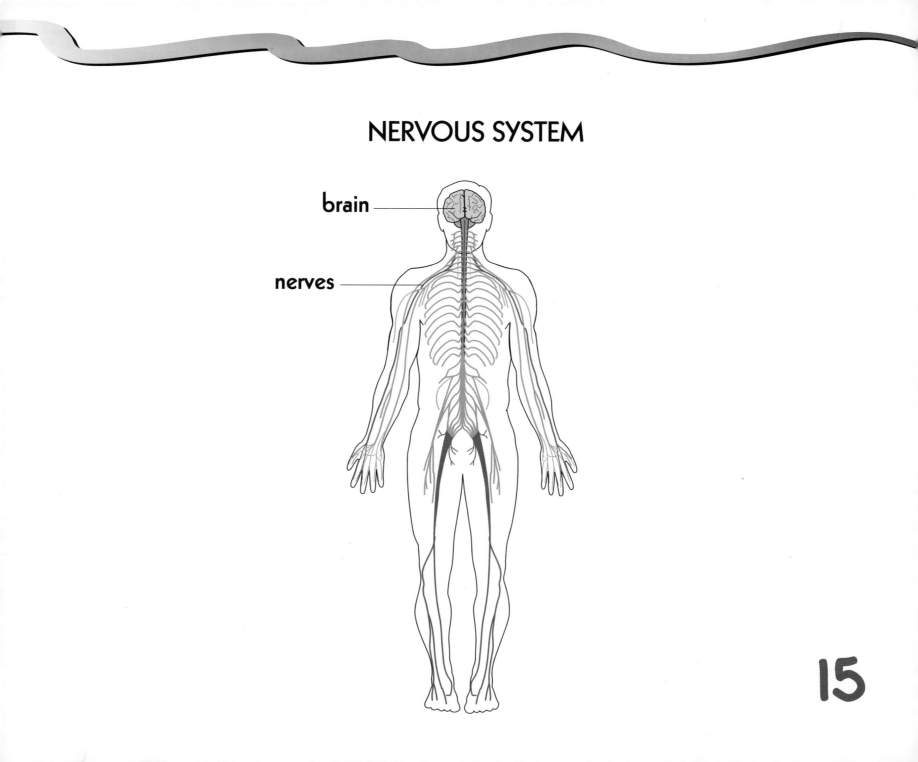

brain

nerves

15

Parts of Your Brain

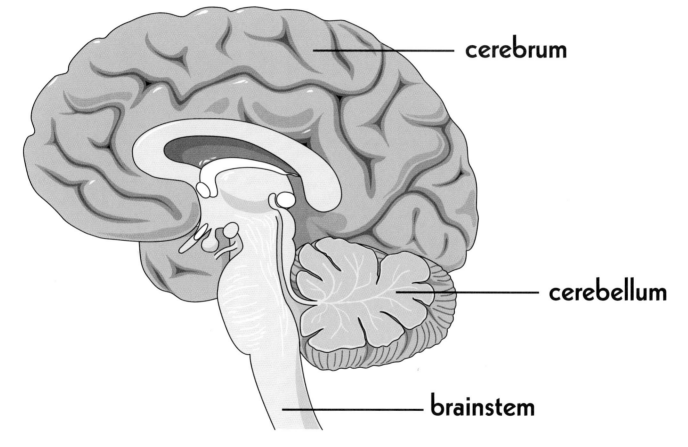

cerebrum

cerebellum

brainstem

Your brain has two main parts. The biggest part is called the **cerebrum** (seh-REE-brum). The cerebrum controls your thinking and the way you make decisions. It also controls your memory, emotions, and imagination. Intuition uses these three things—memory, emotions, and imagination.

Behind and below the cerebrum is a smaller part of your brain called the **cerebellum** (seh-reh-BEL-um). The cerebellum helps you keep your balance. It also gets messages from your muscles. All of these things help guide your intuition.

Your Brain and Your Spinal Cord

The **spinal cord** (SPY-nul KORD) is connected to the brain. Your spinal cord is a long, hollow tube and is about as thin as a pencil. It is filled with **fluids** (FLOO-idz) and is protected by your backbone. Your spinal cord connects the nerves in your body to your brain.

Your brain and nerves need food and **oxygen** (AHK-sih-jen) from nearby cells. Your brain and your nervous system will work better when they have both of these things.

18

BRAIN AND SPINAL CORD

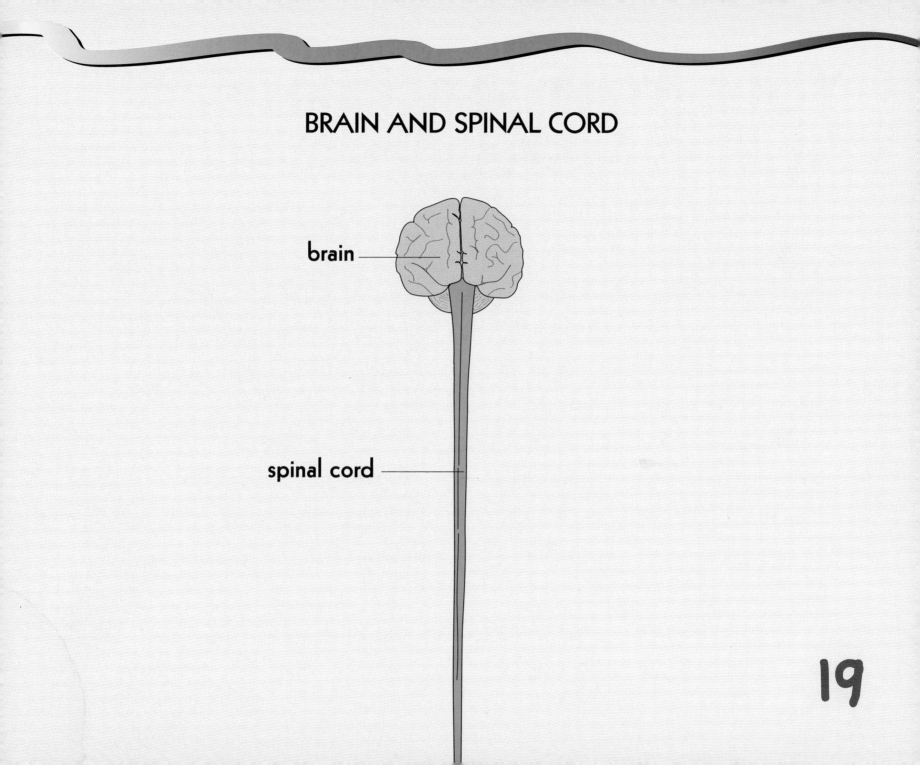

brain

spinal cord

19

Your Brain, Intuition, and Your Health

You may already know that alcohol and drugs are dangerous. They can change the way you think and act. They can also cause you to make bad decisions. But did you know that alcohol and drugs can also hurt your intuition?

The cells of your brain are fragile. Alcohol and drugs are harmful to your brain cells. Staying away from alcohol and drugs, as well as eating foods that are good for you, help to keep your brain and your nervous system healthy. This will also help your sense of intuition.

Your mind and body work together. Your sense of

intuition will also work better when you have plenty of rest and sleep. Sleep, rest, and healthy foods help keep your mind and body healthy.

21

Using Your Intuition

Your intuition can work for you in many ways.

! Let your imagination play with new ideas or new ways to solve problems.

! Do new things and try different activities. Read different kinds of books or play new games. Doing different kinds of things helps stretch your mind and also your sense of intuition.

! If you are having trouble solving a problem, give yourself a rest from the problem for a while. Forget about it for a night and try again the next morning. Your intuition may help you figure it out. And you may wake up with a better feeling about how to solve the problem.

Trust your intuition when it tells you something. Your intuition is working to keep you safe and healthy.

22

Glossary

brain (BRAYN) The main nerve center in your head. Your brain controls everything that your body does.

cerebellum (seh-reh-BEL-um) The smaller part of your brain that is involved with balance and muscle movement.

cerebrum (seh-REE-brum) The biggest part of your brain that controls thinking, decision-making, memory, imagination, and other things.

fluid (FLOO-id) Liquid.

insight (IN-syt) Being able to understand a situation.

instinct (IN-stinkt) Knowing or understanding something based on feelings instead of thoughts.

intuition (in-too-ISH-un) Knowing or figuring out something by relying on a strong feeling or sense.

nerve (NERV) A bundle of rope-like cells that sends messages to and from your brain.

neuron (NUR-on) A brain cell.

oxygen (AHK-sih-jen) A colorless gas that forms part of the air we breathe.

senses (SEN-sez) The ways your body learns what is happening to you and the world around you.

spinal cord (SPY-nul KORD) The thin cord of nerves that runs from the brain through the middle of the back. It carries messages to and from the brain and throughout the body.

Index